Love Your Life
in 30 Days

Love Your Life in 30 Days

The Essential Companion to the Free Online Video Course

Mike Dooley

Hope Koppelman

TUT Publishing
Orlando, FL

To everyone who has a dream
and the courage to pursue it.

TUT Publishing
A division of TUT Enterprises, Inc.
Orlando, FL. www.tut.com

The quotes used throughout this workbook are written by Mike Dooley
and come from the *Notes from the Universe* messages.

Written by Mike Dooley and Hope Koppelman.
Designed by Gina Tyquiengco.

ISBN: 978-0-9814-6029-1
Library of Congress: 2016914108

Printed in the United States of America.

10 9 8 7 6 5 4 3 2 1

Contents

CONTENTS

The Purpose of This Workbook

The purpose of this workbook is to support you on your journey to creating major life transformation. Inside you'll find 30 activities that are designed to help you move closer to living your dreams, whatever they may be, such as writing your first novel, living a healthier lifestyle, tackling that creative project you've been fantasizing about forever, or launching your new business. Even if you don't have a specific dream or goal that you're working toward, by the time you complete these activities you will have:

- A clearer understanding of what you really want.
- An expanded awareness of how the Universe works.
- A deeper perspective on manifestation and your role in it.
- A daily practice that puts what you're passionate about at the forefront of your life.
- Tools that will help you in the days, months, and years ahead.

Each activity takes less than 10 minutes to complete. Our belief is that by the time you complete all 30 activities, you will feel more confident, more capable, and more prepared to live the life of your dreams from here on out.

For extra inspiration each day, sign up for the *Notes from the Universe* messages—daily emails personalized with your name, goals, and dreams, designed to remind you that you have, indeed, been given dominion over all things. Sign up for free at www.tut.com.

How to Get Started

1. COMPLETE ONE ACTIVITY EACH DAY FOR THE NEXT 30 DAYS.
Starting with Day 1, complete one activity each day for the next 30 days. Set aside a few minutes every morning when you wake up or during your lunch break or before you go to bed at night. Each activity takes 10 minutes or less to complete. If you miss a day, no problem, just pick up where you left off when you're ready to return.

2. WATCH THE CORRESPONDING FREE VIDEO TIPS FOR EACH ACTIVITY.
Each activity features a short video lesson that can be accessed online. In these videos, Mike Dooley shares tips and advice relating to each activity, including some of his own personal life stories and experiences. These videos are designed to give you a deeper look into the activities and offer additional inspiration and insights.

To access these videos go to: **www.tut.com/loveyourlife**
Enter the password: **30days**

3. WRITE DOWN YOUR THOUGHTS AND INSIGHTS ABOUT EACH ACTIVITY.
Following each activity in this workbook, you will find a blank page where you can write down any thoughts, ideas, and insights that you have while completing the activity. We suggest spending several minutes each day reflecting on what that day's activity meant to you.

DAY 1

Get Clear About Your Priorities

Est. time: **5 minutes**

Write down at least 5 *general areas* of your life that you want to create change in and develop over the next year. Keeping your goals for change general is powerful because it gives the Universe power to orchestrate the details and figure out "how" your goals can manifest in the best way possible. On Day 3 you will have the chance to "dress up" these generalities with the juicy details that excite you!

Here are some examples of general areas for change:

- Happiness
- Health
- Love
- Friendship
- Creativity
- Spirituality
- Adventure
- Abundance

TIPS

TRY THIS:
Close your eyes and see if you can feel what one (or more) of these areas will feel like once you are thriving in it.

NOTICE:
Have you already started working on developing any of these areas in your life? If so, how?

GOING FORWARD:
Whenever you think in terms of a specific goal, ask yourself what "general area" it falls into: happiness, health, love, etc. See if this gives you a broader perspective on what you really want.

5 general life areas where I want to create change:

1.

2.

3.

4.

5.

Thoughts and insights about Day 1

*Don't be afraid to go where you've never gone and do what you've never done,
because both are necessary to have what you've never had and be who you've never been.*

The Universe

DAY 2

Create Your Theme(s)
Est. time: **7 minutes**

Creating a theme helps you to nail down, stylize, and get excited about the changes that will soon be sweeping through your life. Choose a theme that resonates with you and write it down, using words that have special meaning to you. You may even wish to base it on one or more of your general areas for change from Day 1. Explain your theme's importance and all of its fun ramifications. For example, if your theme is *adventure* that might mean: travel, trying new things, meeting new people, taking chances, exploring new places, leaving your comfort zone, and saying yes to new opportunities. You can even write down several themes and what each one means to you.

Here are some theme ideas:

- International world traveler
- Healthy, happy, and thriving
- Adventure, exploration, discovery
- Overflowing with abundance
- Living limitless and free
- Peace, harmony, and tranquility
- Living life to the fullest each day
- Making a difference in the world
- Creatively inspired and fulfilled
- Spiritually empowered
- The best year of my life
- Happily in love and loved

Tips

Try this:
Use exciting adjectives and flowery words. Perhaps, choose something symbolic to represent each of your themes (a piece of jewelry, a book, a photograph, a quote, a poem). This will give you a physical reminder of your theme.

Notice:
Are these themes new or have you thought about them before?

Going forward:
Can you turn your theme(s) into an affirmation or mantra for easy repitition all year long? (We'll talk more about affirmations and mantras on Day 10.)

My theme:

What my theme means to me:

Symbol:

Optional theme #2:

What my theme means to me:

Symbol:

Optional theme #3:

What my theme means to me:

Symbol:

Thoughts and insights about Day 2

*Has it occurred to you that you could ask for more? Not just more than
you now have, but more than you're now asking for?*

The Universe

DAY 3

Get into the Details and Create a Sense of Excitement

Est. time: **9 minutes**

On Day 1 you wrote down 5 *general areas* of your life where you want to create change over the next year. Now, let those general goals lead you to discover the specific details that excite you—the juicy, sexy, wonderful details that make your heart pound! This will ramp up your emotional connection to the goals you have. Make a list of the details that will be drawn into your life once those goals have manifested. Consider what you'll see, what you'll hear, and what you'll feel. This activity is like creating a visionboard, only using words instead of pictures.

Here are some examples (feel free to go into much greater detail):

ABUNDANCE	RELATIONSHIP	HEALTH	TRAVEL	CREATIVITY
Peace of mind	Best friends	Daily exercise	Exploration	Writing/painting
Free time	Treasured intimacy	Healthy cooking/eating	Meeting new people	Inspiring others
Lots of travel				Self-expression
	Space and independence	Strength and confidence	Peace and serenity	

TIPS

TRY THIS:
Close your eyes and imagine the details you write down (remember to incorporate all your senses: sight, sound, smell, taste, touch, and feel).

NOTICE:
Is there anything you can do this week to "get into" and sample these details? If so, what?

GOING FORWARD:
Pencil some of these details into your calendar (or things you can do to create these details) and start making space for them in your life.

The details I'm excited to create:

Goal 1: ....

Details: ....

....

....

Goal 2: ....

Details: ....

....

....

Goal 3: ....

Details: ....

....

....

Goal 4: ....

Details: ....

....

....

Goal 5: ....

Details: ....

....

....

Thoughts and insights about Day 3

Can you imagine the joy, the peace, the complete sense of satisfaction? The harmony, the love, and stitches of laughter? Can you imagine the interest income?! Good, because nothing else shapes mountains, people, and bank accounts quite like imagination.

The Universe

DAY 4

Showcase Your Inspiration
Est. time: **5 minutes**

It's important to create visual reminders of the goals you're working toward. When you see a reminder of your goals in front of you each day, it starts to become a part of your reality. What reminders can you set up around your office, in your bedroom, on your refrigerator or bathroom mirror? Put something (or several things) up that will inspire you in the days and weeks ahead.

Here are some ideas:

- Hang up your list of priorities from Day 1.
- Hang up a photo or a quote that inspires you.
- Program your phone or computer to send you a positive reminder each day.
- Set your computer or phone wallpaper to an image that inspires you.
- Write a reminder to yourself: to be adventurous, to try something new each day, to channel loving energy into everything you do.
- Make a visionboard with images of the life you want to create.

TIPS

TRY THIS:
Set up reminders in places where you spend the most time: at your desk, on your computer, in your bedroom, on your phone, in your car.

NOTICE:
How does seeing a visual reminder each day change the way you think and feel?

GOING FORWARD:
Change the visual reminders around you whenever you start to become desensitized to them.

Write a list of ways you will showcase your inspiration and choose *at least* one to do right now:

Thoughts and insights about Day 4

Really, all one has to do to transform their life is remind themselves to think and behave a little bit differently each day.

The Universe

DAY 5

Visualize - Imagine a Day in the Life You Dream of Living

Est. time: **5 minutes**

Close your eyes for five minutes and imagine a typical day in the near future, once your priority areas for transformation have come to pass in the most exciting of ways (don't worry about *how* such changes came to be). Imagine the sights, sounds, feelings, and conversations from such a day. Imagine how you feel when you wake up. Imagine celebrating. Imagine explaining the transformation to your friends. Imagine the sense of inner peace you will feel. Imagine where you might live. Imagine where you might vacation. Imagine what you might do for fun. Imagine what your new priorities for change will be. Imagine what your new challenges will be. Imagine all of it as if you are *already living* the life of your dreams.

Tips

Try this:

When you visualize, sit in a comfortable chair, perhaps in a dark and quiet room, to minimize any distractions.

Notice:

How does it feel to visualize? Do you feel any different after visualizing?

Going forward:

Practice visualizing for 5 minutes a day and observe how your feelings change each time.

Before you visualize, write down what you might see and feel:

What a typical day looks like:

The feelings I will have:

Thoughts and insights about Day 5

As surely as the snow falls, the winds rage, and the rivers run, so are you, minute by minute, day by day, inevitably drawn to all your heart desires. Act on this.

The Universe

DAY 6

Take Baby Steps
Toward Your Goals

Est. time: **6 minutes**

This activity is about planning which baby steps you can start taking in the direction of your goals. Choose one of your goals and write it down on the following page, then beneath it write down *at least* 7 baby steps that you can start taking to move toward it. Ask yourself: What else can I try? Where else can I go? Who else can I talk to? You can do this for all of your goals on a separate sheet of paper if you like. Starting in the days and weeks ahead, begin to put these steps into practice.

My goal:

7 baby steps I will take:

1.

2.

3.

4.

5.

6.

7.

Thoughts and insights about Day 6

The secret behind miracles is that the person performing them begins without any knowledge whatsoever of exactly how they will succeed... yet still they begin.

The Universe

DAY 7

Play Detective - Observe Your Thoughts, Words, and Actions

Est. time: **5 minutes**

The activities leading up to Day 7 have all dealt with pro-actively creating transformation. Now, it's time to go on the defense by observing your thoughts, words, and actions. When you play detective in this way, you can quickly stem the tide of any self-made negativity that may cross your wires or contradict the initiatives you're taking to spark change. Simply observe all that you're thinking, saying, and physically doing. This will help you to understand some of your subliminal inner messaging. When you don't like what you're thinking, saying, or doing, then deliberately and lovingly craft a counter-message to immediately put to use.

TIPS

TRY THIS:
If you're not sure how to lovingly craft a counter-message, simply say, "I choose…" (and fill in the blank). "I choose to experience feelings of peace." "I choose to bring myself into the present moment." "I choose to love myself."

NOTICE:
Was it easy to spot any negative thoughts, words, and actions? Did it get easier with practice?

GOING FORWARD:
Continue with this practice until the day arrives when you become your own best friend instead of your harshest critic.

Thoughts I observed:

Counter-message:

Words I observed:

Counter-message:

Actions I observed:

Counter-message:

Thoughts and insights about Day 7

Reframe every thought, word, and action from the perspective of the person you've always dreamed you'd be, as if your life was already as you've always dreamed it would be.

The Universe

DAY 8

Identify and Change a Story You Tell

Est. time: **10 minutes**

Sometimes we get so caught up in the stories we tell ourselves and others that before long these stories become our truth (or what we believe is our truth). We often justify or explain or make excuses for how and why we are the way we are—perhaps even how and why we aren't further along than we are. To change our truth, we simply have to change the stories we tell and believe. Pay attention to the stories you're telling, and if you hear a story that isn't serving you and your highest good, start telling a new story that serves you better.

TIPS

TRY THIS:

Take into consideration the stories you tell about various aspects of your life: work, relationships, happiness, creativity, money. You can re-write any or all of these stories that aren't serving you.

NOTICE:

Who are you telling your stories to? Would it also help them to hear you tell a new story?

GOING FORWARD:

Start telling stories that excite you, thrill you, humor you, and fill you with joy. Let them be open-ended, leaving room for infinite possibilities.

Re-write your story by answering the following questions:

What old story have you been telling that isn't serving you? How does this story make you feel?

What new story will you begin telling? How does this story make you feel?

Thoughts and insights about Day 8

For whatever you do to further your dreams,
I will do more for you.

The Universe

DAY 9

Choose Beliefs for Each Area
You Wish to Transform

Est. time: **8 minutes**

Our beliefs are powerful. It's our beliefs that determine what we think, what we say, and what we do, at any given moment, thus creating our reality. Choose beliefs that serve you in each area of your life that you wish to transform: health, career, relationship, creativity, etc., and/or jot down some *general beliefs* that will have an impact on the whole of your life. They don't have to be beliefs that you already possess, they can be beliefs that you'd like to possess going forward.

Here are some examples:

- I believe I am protected, guided, and loved; always in the right place at the right time.
- I believe everything that happens and everything that doesn't happen adds to who I am. Everything is setting me up for greatness.
- I believe I naturally attract the right people who add to my life, as I add to theirs.
- I believe the Universe has my back and is pressing out to me all that I desire.

Beliefs that serve me in the areas I wish to transform:

Thoughts and insights about Day 9

You want what you want because you know it's possible. If it wasn't, you wouldn't.
This is powerful. Embrace it. For whatever else you believe or don't believe,
this belief alone can take you the distance.

The Universe

TIPS

TRY THIS:

Practice repeating your affirmation at the same time each day (every morning when you wake up, each night before you go to sleep, on your way to work, or whenever you need a reminder).

NOTICE:

Your words contain great power. Can you feel it as you repeat your affirmations?

GOING FORWARD:

Choose a new affirmation each day or week or month. You can write several on a small sheet of paper, put them in a bowl, and randomly choose a new one when you're ready for a change. Also, perhaps revisit the Going Forward instructions for Day 2: Create Your Theme(s).

My affirmation for each area I wish to transform:

Area:

Affirmation:

Area:

Affirmation:

Area:

Affirmation:

Thoughts and insights about Day 10

You know you've made it when you suddenly realize that there's nothing in the world anyone might ever give you, no matter how grand or fabulous, that you can't give to yourself.

The Universe

DAY 11

Surround Yourself with Empowering Resources

Est. time: **10 minutes**

Surrounding yourself with resources that inspire and motivate you is extremely important. There are so many resources that can do this, yet you may not even know that they exist. Do some research and make a list of resources that you can start utilizing in the days, weeks, and months ahead.

Here are some examples:

- Sign up for *Notes from the Universe* daily inspirational emails at www.tut.com.
- Make a reading list. What have you always wanted to read? What's on the *NY Times* Bestseller List? Try TUT's Recommended Reading at tut.com.
- Listen to free podcasts. Elizabeth Gilbert has a podcast called "Magic Lessons," about harnessing creativity. NPR has a series called "Ted Radio Hour," based on TED Talks from the world's most remarkable minds.
- Find websites that are doing great things: TUT (check out our blog), Brain Pickings, TED, Huffington Post Good News Stories.
- Find groups in your area that support your vision. Try Meetup.com, where you can connect with like-minded people or Creative Mornings, a breakfast lecture series in cities around the world.

TIPS

TRY THIS:
Ask your friends what inspiring resources they recommend. You'll be surprised how many great resources you find when you ask people their favorite websites, podcasts, books, and groups.

NOTICE:
Is there anyone you know who would benefit from the resources you've written down? If so, pass it on! When you find a resource you love, tell a friend and inspire someone else.

GOING FORWARD:
Circle several ideas from your list and start exploring them right away.

My empowering resources:

Thoughts and insights about Day 11

It only takes one idea, one second in time, one friend, one dream,
one leap of faith, to change everything, forever.

The Universe

DAY 12

Plan Your Celebration
Est. time: **10 minutes**

How will you celebrate your transformation once some of your dreams start coming true? Write a celebration plan. Get into the nitty-gritty details, and when your dreams start to manifest, honor and reward yourself with this celebration.

Here are some ideas:

- Throw a party. Who will you invite? Where will you host it? What will you say during your toast?
- Take a trip. Where will you go? What will you do? Who will you take with you?
- Purchase something special. What will you get? Where will you get it? What will you do with it?
- Send thank you cards or gifts to the people who helped you. Who will you send them to? What will you send? What will you thank them for?

TIPS

TRY THIS:
Create a visual reminder of your plan to inspire you (a photo or some other symbol of your celebration).

NOTICE:
Are there any smaller milestones you can also celebrate along the way?

GOING FORWARD:
Once all of these celebrations have wrapped up, who will you help to achieve what you have achieved? How?

My celebration plan:

Thoughts and insights about Day 12

There are really only two conditions of the human experience: very, very happy or about to become very, very happy. Which are you today?

The Universe

DAY 13

Random Acts of Kindness
Est. time: **5 minutes**

This activity is about spreading love and bringing joy to others. Write down several ways that you can spread love and bring joy into people's lives, whether it's making someone laugh or volunteering your time to help someone in need. Throughout your day, look for opportunities to show the people around you (whether friends or strangers) they're special, loved, worthy, important, and valued.

Here are some ideas:

- Pay someone's bill.
- Smile first when crossing paths with a stranger.
- Call a friend just because.
- Buy a co-worker coffee.
- Pick up garbage that isn't yours.
- Leave a large tip, twice the norm.
- Leave a note on someone's car.
- Write a card to a friend.
- Give someone a compliment.
- Leave extra coins in the parking meter.

TIPS

TRY THIS:
Treat yourself to acts of kindness as well (you can even make a separate list that's specifically oriented to you).

NOTICE:
Is it even necessary to receive credit for your actions in order to feel good about them?

GOING FORWARD:
Write down various acts of kindness on small pieces of paper, put them in a bowl, and choose a random one each day.

Today's random acts of kindness:

Thoughts and insights about Day 13

You just never know who in the crowd, standing beside you in line, or passing you on the street, might be raised in spirit or even lifted from despair by the kindness in your glance and the comfort of your smile.

The Universe

DAY 14

Create a Mock Calendar
or Daily Planner

Est. time: **10 minutes**

Find a calendar or planner and fill certain days of certain months with wonderful events, trips, parties, dates, and adventures that you want to create for yourself in the year ahead. This is a fun way to get creative and envision new things unfolding in your life. After you've filled in the days, hang it up to remind yourself of the exciting things you're going to create and experience in the year ahead.

Here are some ideas:

- Events: workshops, gallery openings, concerts, museums, festivals.
- Trips: a month in Spain, camping on the beach, a romantic getaway.
- Appointments: book signings, meetings with editor, speaking engagements.
- Dates: dinner under the stars, dancing, hiking, picnics in the park.
- Special Occasions: parties with friends, holidays with family, New Year's Eve in New York.
- Adventures: moving to another city, sky-diving, learning to scuba dive.
- Classes: language, yoga, art, dance, photography.

TIPS

TRY THIS:
Find some events that really are happening around town and add them to your list.

NOTICE:
Did you pencil in "down time" to relax or read or rest?

GOING FORWARD:
Now that you know the types of things you want to be doing, take action to make them happen.

Write your ideas below and then add them to a calendar or planner:

Events:

Trips:

Appointments:

Dates:

Special Occasions:

Adventures:

Classes:

Thoughts and insights about Day 14

Would you believe that there are some people who actually think they can change their life through "pretending it better"? Yep, and we call them masters.

The Universe

DAY 15

Send Thoughts of Love
Est. time: **5 minutes**

Send them love! Imagine loved ones in need and send them mental hugs or comfort on wings, as if you had an endless supply of angels on standby, awaiting your marching orders. Send thoughts of love, blessings, and peace to people as you go about your day—the stranger in the elevator, your co-workers, the cashier at the grocery store, your boss, the homeless person on the street corner, the driver who cuts you off in traffic. If you see something that disappoints you, instead of reacting with anger, send a blessing: "Be careful brother or sister, I love you." "Angels, please keep this person safe." "May light and love surround you." You don't have to say a single word, the people around you will feel your energy and love.

Tips

Try this:
Send thoughts of love when it's easy and when it's hard; when you see things that make you happy and when you see things that make you sad.

Notice:
How does sending love to others affect your own sense of inner peace and happiness?

Going forward:
Once a day, or more, practice sending love to someone in need of support. You can also send love to specific situations, countries in conflict, or the planet as a whole. And don't forget to send yourself love as well.

To whom will you send love:

3 people you love:

1.

2.

3.

3 people who upset you:

1.

2.

3.

3 people you admire or are grateful for:

1.

2.

3.

Thoughts and insights about Day 15

Here's a tip on how to bring absolute joy into your life faster than it may have otherwise arrived: every day, in some small way, even secretly if you like, look for a chance to help someone else.

The Universe

DAY 16

Discover Rituals that Serve You
Est. time: **5 minutes**

A ritual is an observance or practice that is performed the same way each time. We perform rituals every day, whether we realize it or not—brushing our teeth, taking a shower, eating meals, are all rituals that contribute to our health and well-being. There is evidence that rituals, even simple rituals, can have a profound effect on how we feel about ourselves. Choose a new ritual to perform. Let this be a ritual that you can easily maintain in the weeks ahead, something small that contributes to your overall sense of peace and happiness.

Here are some ideas:

- Light a candle or incense on behalf of someone or to celebrate something new each day.
- Meditate or pray for a few minutes each day.
- Visualize your life as you want it to be.
- Do some stretching or breathing exercises.
- Read a page from a book each night before you fall asleep.
- Go outside and look at the stars each night.
- Give thanks for the good things in your day through a gratitude journal.

TIPS

TRY THIS:
Set a special space for your ritual to take place. Set out anything you may need in advance: photographs, books, journal, incense.

NOTICE:
What time of day or night works best to perform your ritual(s)? Perhaps, first thing when you wake up or before you go to sleep each night?

GOING FORWARD:
Try creating a new ritual each week or each month until you find what fits your life the best.

Rituals that may be ideal for me:

Thoughts and insights about Day 16

Do you know what you have in common with the tiniest percentage of human beings
who have ever, ever, ever graced the face of the earth? You can still walk barefoot.
You can still pick flowers. You can still make a difference.

The Universe

DAY 17

Acknowledge Your Amazing Self and Past Successes

Est. time: **10 minutes**

It's common to look at our lives and see what's not working, what we want to change, and what we think could be better. But how often do we look at our lives and acknowledge all of the wonderful things that have worked, that have gone right, and that are amazing just the way they are? Instead of looking at what's missing from your life, look at all the wonderful things that have already manifested for you. Make a list of the goals and dreams you once had that have now come true. For fun, include some of your present goals and dreams that you now have *as if they have already come true*. This way, you will see your present goals and dreams with the ones that have already manifested, in the same light.

TIPS

TRY THIS:
Include goals and dreams you've manifested in different areas of your life: education, career, family, friendship, love, creativity, spirituality, travel, education, hobbies, skills.

NOTICE:
Did you consider goals and dreams that are both big and small? You're not limited to big dreams only. Consider your health for instance: even with some ailments, 99% of your body most likely functions effortlessly and pain free. That's worth celebrating!

GOING FORWARD:
Express gratitude out loud each day for all that works so magically in your life.

My goals and dreams that have already manifested:

Thoughts and insights about Day 17

When in a hurry, step one for changing the entire world is falling in love with it as it already is. Same for changing yourself. And best of all, with this approach, there is no step two.

The Universe

DAY 18

Script a Day in Your Future Life as if it Were Your Present Life

Est. time: **10 minutes**

Write a brief script depicting a day in your future life once your dreams have *already come to pass*, which you can later visualize. Include a number of elements that imply your happiness. What would a wonderful day look like? Would you kiss your partner good morning when you wake up? Would you wake the children for school? Would you eat breakfast in bed? Would you spend the day creating in your studio? Would you take a walk in nature? Would you meet a friend for lunch? Would you invite all your friends to join you for a special dinner? Write down the highlights of your day and when you're done, breeze through it in your mind, as if you were watching your life play out on the silver screen.

TIPS

TRY THIS:
Include everything that will bring you joy and don't worry about whether it's realistic.

NOTICE:
Is there anything in your script that you can do right now?

GOING FORWARD:
Revisit your script periodically. Perhaps, keep a copy of it in your journal or tape it to your bathroom mirror. Update it from time to time, as necessary.

How a day in my future life looks:

Thoughts and insights about Day 18

Live your dreams now, to any degree that you can. With every purchase. Every decision. Every hello and goodbye. Every assignment. Every conversation. Every meal. Every morning, afternoon, and evening. And never, ever, ever look back.

The Universe

DAY 19

Imagine How Your Dreams Will Benefit Others

Est. time: **8 minutes**

We often imagine how we will benefit once our dreams come true, but we rarely imagine how our friends and loved ones will benefit once our dreams come true. Choose two or three people in your life who deeply love you, and imagine how your happiness and success will impact their lives. How proud they will feel of you. What they will learn from your courage. What it might inspire them to do.

TRY THIS:
*Think about the gratitude
and appreciation your
loved ones will express
about you in conversations
with others.*

NOTICE:
*Are you more inspired
now to achieve your
dreams?*

GOING FORWARD:
*Give yourself credit for
having dreams and goals
that will help more people
than just yourself. Let this
motivate you as much
as your own growth
and happiness.*

Loved ones who will benefit and be enriched from my success and happiness:

Name:

Benefits:

Name:

Benefits:

Name:

Benefits:

Name:

Benefits:

Thoughts and insights about Day 19

When you move toward a dream, it moves toward you.
When you move every day, it moves every day.

The Universe

DAY 20

Meet Your Future Peers
Est. time: **9 minutes**

Who do you know that has accomplished what you now dream of accomplishing? Make a list of 10 to 20 names, and somewhere within that list include your own name. This simple process of associating your name with theirs will remind you that what they've done, anyone, *including you,* can do. They started out where you started out—a novice, a dreamer. We're all made of the same stuff, the most significant difference between us is our thoughts, words, beliefs and actions. And these can be changed, experimented with, and chosen in ways that serve us. Make your list, have fun, imagine "rubbing shoulders" with these future peers, and the day will come when others, inspired by you, will include your name on their list.

TIPS

TRY THIS:

Think of these people in the context of a common social setting you enjoy, like having a meal together, playing golf, or going on vacation.

NOTICE:

How might you one day help them as much as they help you? With insights, advice, comfort?

GOING FORWARD:

Learn from the people on your list. Learn their stories, read their autobiographies, explore the paths they took to get to where they are.

My future peers, pals, and buddies:

1.

2.

3.

4.

5.

6.

7.

8.

9.

10.

11.

12.

13.

14.

15.

16.

17.

18.

19.

20.

Thoughts and insights about Day 20

*Folks are often so mesmerized by the gold medals, trophies, and daunting heights
they aspire to, they tend to forget that their heroes and heroines, more often than not,
started with far less than they now have.*

The Universe

DAY 21

Speak of Your Success
With a Friend

Est. time: **10 minutes**

This activity requires a friend, on the phone or in person, who understands your way of seeing the world. If no friend is available, try it with an imaginary friend or your own reflection in the mirror. The goal is for the two (or more) of you to celebrate as if your present dreams have *already come true*. Speak about your dreams in the past or present tense. If you go first, speak about the success of your own dreams, and then congratulate your friend(s) on their successes. After you've spoken for a few minutes, then allow your friend(s) to do the same, speaking of their own dreams coming true, and then speaking of your successes. Get into the elaborate details of all the expected and unexpected consequences that have come from the successes in each of your lives.

TIPS

TRY THIS:
Imagine that the dreams you're talking about came true many months ago.

NOTICE:
Was it challenging, fun, powerful to imagine the real consequences that will spring from your future success?

GOING FORWARD:
As you do this more and more, be sure to imagine and discuss not only the positive consequences on your future, but also some of the new challenges you face.

Write down the highlights of your conversation.

Share about your success:

Share about your friend's success:

Thoughts and insights about Day 21

Great big, innovative, world changing ideas are plentiful.
People who take tiny little baby steps toward them are rare.

The Universe

DAY 22

List 20 Things You Love to Do
Est. time: **8 minutes**

This is a simple activity to remind you of the things *already in your life* that thrill you the most. Write down 20 things you love to do (from the simplest thing, like drinking a cup of tea in the morning… to the most exotic, like backpacking in a foreign country). You might be surprised to realize how many you already do each day.

Here are some ideas:

- Morning coffee.
- Practicing yoga.
- Taking a walk.
- Meditating.
- Being in nature.
- Curling up with a good book.
- Watching the sun rise or set.

TIPS

TRY THIS:
Circle all of the things on your list that you can do today, and do them.

NOTICE:
What has kept you from doing some of the easier things on your list?

GOING FORWARD:
Write down each of the things on your list on a small sheet of paper and put them into a bowl. Draw a random one (or more) each day and treat yourself to it.

20 things I love to do:

1.
2.
3.
4.
5.
6.
7.
8.
9.
10.
11.
12.
13.
14.
15.
16.
17.
18.
19.
20.

Thoughts and insights about Day 22

*Just wanted to formally announce that the world is indeed
ready for ALL of you. Go on.*

The Universe

DAY 23

Express Gratitude
Est. time: **8 minutes**

Gratitude is powerful. It's an expression of thankfulness and appreciation for all you have and all you are. Plus, expressing gratitude is the same as expressing the sentiment, "I have received," which is a powerful declaration on this plane of manifestation. You can therefore express gratitude for the things you have, and thereby attract more, and you can express gratitude for the things you don't yet have, *as if you already had them*, to thereby attract them. Write down 15 things (tangible or intangible) that are already in your life that you are grateful for, and then list 5 more that you will soon be grateful for, as if you already had them.

TIPS

TRY THIS:
Consider what's most important to you and start your list there.

NOTICE:
Are there any people on your list who you can thank? If so, send them an email or write them a note or call them to tell them how much you appreciate them.

GOING FORWARD:
Create a simple daily gratitude practice. Here's one idea: Before you go to bed each night, think of 3 things that happened in the past 24 hours that you're grateful for and/or 3 things that will happen in the next 24 hours that you're grateful for (in advance).

15 things I am grateful for:

1.
2.
3.
4.
5.
6.
7.
8.
9.
10.
11.
12.
13.
14.
15.

5 things I will be grateful for:

1.
2.
3.
4.
5.

Thoughts and insights about Day 23

There's no such thing as too much gratitude. Because the more of it you express, the more reasons you'll be given to express it.

The Universe

DAY 24

Write Yourself a Letter from an Admirer

Est. time: **8 minutes**

How often do you take the time to see yourself from another person's perspective? Give it a try. Pretend that you are someone else—one of your many friends, a loved one, a co-worker, a business partner—and write a letter as that person showering YOU with praise, love, and appreciation. There's a reason why your friends and family love you as much as they do. See yourself from their perspective!

Here are some things you might include:

- Why you're such a great friend/sibling/parent/child/partner.
- What you bring to this world that's unique to you.
- Why you're an inspiration to so many people.
- What people love most about you.

Tips

TRY THIS:
Think about how you make other people feel about themselves, and include that in your letter.

NOTICE:
Was it easy or hard to see yourself from someone else's perspective?

GOING FORWARD:
Be the admirer to someone else. Write a letter to someone you love telling them all the reasons why you admire them.

Dear   ,

Thoughts and insights about Day 24

Everyone's a giant, everyone's powerful, everyone's trying, everyone's learning, everyone's worthy, everyone's loved, and everyone... loves you.

The Universe

DAY 25

Set an Intention for Your Day

Est. time: **5 minutes**

Setting an intention is a powerful practice. Essentially, all intentions are clear forms of "end results" we wish to achieve and dreams we wish to manifest. Moreover, given the immediacy of our intentions, they bypass our fears of *how* they will manifest and throw us into action instantaneously. Set an intention and allow it to guide your thoughts, words, and actions in its light. As you move through your day, call on your intention to guide you in every way.

Here are some ideas of intentions you might set:

- Be present and enjoy each moment.
- Bring love to every word I speak to myself and others.
- Consciously care about what others are feeling.
- Find the good in any unexpected setback.
- Start writing my book.
- Create an online dating profile.
- Commit to starting a new health routine.

TIPS

TRY THIS:
Shift your focus back to your intention whenever you get distracted (you may even want to carry a physical reminder with you: a stone, a coin, your intention written down on paper).

NOTICE:
How does having an intention change the thoughts you think, the words you speak, and your actions throughout the day?

GOING FORWARD:
Set an intention each time you want to practice bringing more awareness to a situation.

My intention for today:

Intentions I may consider in the days ahead:

Thoughts and insights about Day 25

What wouldn't you give to live, love, and be happy, deliriously happy, forevermore?
Well, that's just it, you needn't give anything. Just decide to live, love, and be happy,
deliriously happy, from this moment forward.

The Universe

DAY 26

Put Your Manifestation Skills to Work

Est. time: **6 minutes**

Choose something small that you want to manifest and then do everything in your power to manifest it, while allowing the Universe to do everything in its power to bring it to you. Mentally see it, and then physically make space for it. To manifest a smile from a stranger, vibrate that desire into the world. See it done in your mind and imagine receiving it. Then, go outside, smile, say hello, do your part. To manifest an invitation to an event, let your friends know you're free that weekend, make some phone calls, send some messages, find out what's going on around town. This activity reminds us that our actions are an essential part of the manifestation process. We must do *all we can* in order for the Universe to do *all it can*.

Here are some ideas of things to manifest:

- A smile from a stranger.
- A feather.
- A free tea/coffee.
- A compliment.
- An invitation to an event.
- A phone call from someone.

Today I want to manifest:

Things I can do to increase the chances of it happening:

(while leaving room for magic from the universe)

Thoughts and insights about Day 26

Get out, get out, get out even more! Because there are people you've yet to meet, laughs you've yet to share, stories you've yet to live, and riches you've yet to tap, that will not find you under any other circumstances.

The Universe

DAY 27

Write an "I Rock" List
Est. time: **7 minutes**

This activity is about celebrating yourself. Write an "I rock" list to celebrate your own accomplishments, character, charm, wit, transparency, beauty, strength, and savoir-faire, as well as the progress you're making in all areas of your life. If you're feeling clever, include some "I rocks" for things that you will soon "rock for," as if you've *already accomplished them*. For example, "I rock for writing my first novel! I rock for finding love! I rock for traveling to over 20 countries!"

Here are some examples:

- I rock for finding beauty in every situation.
- I rock for nourishing my body with healthy, delicious food each day.
- I rock for the amazing friends and family I have.
- I rock for my positivity and strength and compassion.
- I rock for helping people to see what's great about themselves.

TIPS

TRY THIS:

Include some things you now rock for and some things you will soon rock for in the future.

NOTICE:

Are there still many, many more reasons why you rock, in addition to what's here?

GOING FORWARD:

Invite a friend or family member to join you and write a "You Rock" list about each other. You might be surprised by some of the reasons why they think you rock.

Celebrate your accomplishments, character, charm, wit, transparency, beauty, strength, and savoir-faire.

I rock _____

I rock _____

I rock _____

I rock _____

I rock _____

I rock _____

I rock _____

I rock _____

I rock _____

I rock _____

I rock _____

I rock _____

Thoughts and insights about Day 27

It is understandably human nature to see yourself as small. Until you stop seeing yourself as just human. You are pure energy: infinite, inexhaustible, and irresistible.

The Universe

DAY 28

Write a Letter to Yourself from Your Future Self

Est. time: **9 minutes**

Write a letter from your future self 5 years down the road to your present self now. Tell yourself about your amazing successes, the dreams of yours that have come true, what you did to achieve them, how your life looks, etc. Write this as if all your current dreams have *already been reached*. If your wiser, future self has a deeper understanding about life, a greater sense of peace and happiness, a clearer vision of what's important, be sure to include that as well.

TIPS

TRY THIS:
Close your eyes for several moments and ask yourself, "What message does my wiser, future self have for my present self?" Be still and listen for the answer.

NOTICE:
Is your wiser, future self more loving? More gentle? More peaceful? More understanding? More joyful? How can you embody these qualities more today?

GOING FORWARD:
When a difficult situation arises, ask yourself what your wiser, future self would do.

Dear amazing, awesome self,

Love,
Your wiser, rocking, future self

Thoughts and insights about Day 28

In your divinely sanctioned quest for having, doing, and being ever more, should you ever need a little inspiration, simply think of all you now have, all you now do, and all you now are.

The Universe

DAY 29

What Your Future Self Wants You to Know Today

Est. time: **6 minutes**

This is another *act as if* activity. Picking up from Day 28, imagine your life 5 years in the future: all you've learned, all you've experienced, and all the changes that have taken place. You are older, wiser, happier, and more at peace. From this perspective, summarize the 5 most important lessons or suggestions that your future self wants your present self to know.

For example:

- Spend more time with family.
- Cherish your friendships.
- Save more money (or spend more money).
- Work harder or smarter or maybe don't work so hard.
- Be more forgiving of yourself and others.
- Don't take things so seriously, lighten up, have fun.

TIPS

TRY THIS:
Keep your list somewhere that you will be reminded of it each day.

NOTICE:
Did you notice that most of these lessons simply require a fresh perspective that can be accessed in the blink of an eye?

GOING FORWARD:
Create an affirmation that claims these lessons have been learned and incorporated into your life (for example: I now live with great love and patience for those in my life).

5 lessons I'm ready to embrace:

1.

2.

3.

4.

5.

Thoughts and insights about Day 29

Don't wait for those feelings of excitement, confidence, and clarity before you take action. Take action first, without them, and they will follow.

The Universe

DAY 30

Reflecting on This Project
Est. time: **10 minutes**

Congratulations! You've made it all the way to Day 30. The following questions will help you reflect on this project and see how it has served you, plus how it will serve you going forward. You can answer any of the questions below or just journal and reflect in your own way.

- In 20 words or less describe how this workbook has helped you.
- What have you learned about yourself through this workbook?
- What are your biggest takeaways?
- How have these activities helped you move closer to your dreams?
- What was your favorite activity and why?
- Which of these activities might you practice in the future?
- Did you find that on most days you had time to complete each activity?

TIPS

TRY THIS:
Consider the upside to continuing some of these activities, and consider if you don't.

NOTICE:
How do you feel now that you've completed all of these activities? Is there a change in your overall sense of happiness, peace, or clarity since you began?

GOING FORWARD:
Make a plan for how you might continue your spiritual practice moving forward.

My reflections on this 30 day project:

Tomorrow I will begin:

Thoughts and insights about Day 30

Now! Go! Stake your claim! Hold out your hands. Move, get ready, give thanks.
Imagine, and let go. Act, and have faith. Persist. Do what you can, when you can, all
you can. Because never again, not in a million years, not over ten thousand lifetimes,
will you ever again be as close as you are today.

The Universe

About the Authors

Mike Dooley is a former PriceWaterhouseCoopers international tax consultant turned entrepreneur. He's the founder of TUT, a philosophical Adventurers Club on the Internet that's now home to over 725,000 members from virtually every country and territory in the world. His inspirational books emphasizing spiritual accountability have been published in 25 languages, and he was one of the featured teachers in the international phenomenon *The Secret*. Today Mike is best known for his free *Notes from the Universe* emailings and his *New York Times* bestsellers *Infinite Possibilities* and *Leveraging the Universe*. Mike lives what he teaches, traveling internationally to speak on life, dreams, and happiness. To learn more visit www.tut.com.

Hope Koppelman is the author of several books for adults and children, including *The Gifts of Writing* and *The Secrets the Earths Keeps*. For over a decade Hope has been leading the creative initiative at TUT, serving as both Creative Director and Senior Editor. She is also a black belt in Tae Kwon Do, a Certified Yoga Instructor, and a life-long student of the Universe, learning to deepen and evolve her awareness of love every day. She spends her time between the mountains in Western North Carolina, the ocean in Florida, and a small village in Southern Spain. To learn more visit www.hopekoppelman.com.